100 MUST DO

Hong Kong

Outdoor Adventures, Fun Things to Do, Festival Calendar, Local Food, Historical Sights, Non-Touristy Places, Unusual Hotels Hostels

Copyright 2018 by Kevin Hampton - All rights reserved.

All rights Reserved. No part of this publication or the information in it may be quoted from or reproduced in any form by means such as printing, scanning, photocopying or otherwise without prior written permission of the copyright holder.

Disclaimer and Terms of Use: Effort has been made to ensure that the information in this book is accurate and complete, however, the author and the publisher do not warrant the accuracy of the information, text, and graphics contained within the book due to the rapidly changing nature of science, research, known and unknown facts and the internet. The Author and the publisher do not hold any responsibility for errors, omissions or contrary interpretation of the subject matter herein. This book is presented solely for motivational and informational purposes only.

Introduction

Hong Kong is a world class city and that means there are world class things to see and do. Here you will find 100 of the best Hong Kong tourist attractions that incorporate the surrounding area. With so many things to see and do in Hong Kong, choosing can be difficult, so why not start with a list of the best, so you can get the most out of your vacation time.

Table of Contents

TO VISIT - Historical and Cultural Sights 5
TO VISIT - What's Happening Festivals Calendar 10
TO VISIT - Night Clubs & Bars 13
TO VISIT - NOT Tourist Places (the Advice of Locals) 16
TO DO - Outdoor Adventures and Nature 20
TO TASTE - Local Food &Cuisine 23
Affordable Cool Cafes and Restaurants 28
TO BUY - Local and Authentic Souvenirs 32
TO STAY - the Best Unusual Hotels and Hostels 35

TO VISIT - Historical and Cultural Sights

Views From the Star Ferry *Special mission!*

If you want to get the best possible views of the iconic skyline Hong Kong offers along Victoria Harbor, get on the Star Ferry at the Tsim Sha Tsui terminal heading to Central terminal. It's one of the cheapest and most rewarding things you'll do. The crossing is only 7-minutes so you don't have a lot of time to get those pictures, but it's truly mesmerizing. Fares range from HK$2.70 to HK$3.70.

Wong Tai Sin Temple

The Wong Tai Sin temple, also known as Huang Chu-ping temple, commemorates the famous monk of Yore, who was born in the 4th century. He went on to become a deity at Heng Shan. Today worshippers pray for good fortunes through their offerings and the worshipping of the sacred portrait of Wong Tai Sin. This is a beautiful structure and on the complex there is also a beautiful and extravagant Good Wish Garden, and some other interesting buildings.

2 Chuk Yuen Village, Wong Tai Sin, Kowloon, Hong Kong, Phone: +852-2327-8141.

Wong Tai Sin Temple, Hong Kong

Victoria Central Business District

Take a wander through the Victoria Central Business District and you'll soon get an understanding of why Hong Kong is one of the greatest international financial hubs on the globe. There are still a few lovely colonial buildings standing in the neighborhood, but for the most part its new skyscrapers rising high into the sky. While strolling here you can visit the famous skyscraper that's the Bank of China, one of the tallest buildings in the world. You'll want to stop at the Zoological and Botanical Gardens and the Man Mo Temple should be on the list too!

Avenue of Stars and Waterfront Promenade

Make sure you visit the Avenue of Stars when you are in Tsim Sha Tsui, which is a promenade dedicated to Chinese Stars, much like the Hollywood Walk of Fame. Stars like Bruce Lee are among the stars. This Avenue of Stars is part of the longer waterfront promenade, a popular spot used by locals jog, walk, and just hang out. In addition, this is where you'll find the Symphony of Light taking place in the harbor nightly. There's so much to enjoy here, don't miss out!

Ocean Park

A day here will give almost all the thrills and excitement you can handle for the day. You get to visit the Grand Aquarium, ride the roller coasters, walk through old Hong Kong, view exotic wildlife, and more. What's really cool is the aquarium dome, which is the largest in the world. Make sure to take part in the Giant Panda Adventure! There's also all kinds of rides like the Raging River. This park ranks up there with Disneyland for the locals. Come enjoy one of the best days ever!

No.180 Wong Chuk Hang Road, Hong Kong, Phone: +852-3923-2323.

Big Buddha – The Tian Tan Buddha Statue

Big Buddha sits up high at the Po Lin Monastery on Lantau Island, and at 34 meters high, you won't be able to miss it. Big Buddha certainly makes an impactful statement, and it is the largest free standing statue in the world that anyone knows about. If you like to get up early, you can climb Lantau Peak with a monk guiding you along the way, and make it to the top in time to watch the sunrise over the islands and surrounding sea. What an experience it is to see Big Buddha.

Po Lin Monastery, Ngong Ping, Lantau Island, Hong Kong, Phone: +86-903-509-4316.

Big Buddha, Ngong Ping Lantau Island, Hong Kong

Tai O Fishing Village *Special mission!*

Tai O Fishing Village offers you an experience like no other in Hong Kong. There are no theme parks, bright city lights, or crowded markets here. Here you will find people that live a quieter more traditional lifestyle. At Tai O live the Tanka people, fisher folk, with homes build on stilts over the tidal flats. The locals will take you on boat rides and you might even see the rare pink dolphin. You can also experience their local market, and the Tai O Royal Committee Historic and Cultural Showroom where you'll find relics from these communities past.

Tai O, Lantau Island, Outlying Islands, Phone: 97114727

Art Museum of the Chinese University of Hong Kong

Located inside the Chinese University in Hong Kong there's no fee to visit the art museum. It's very interesting and you'll see some beautiful pieces of art in many forms. If you love antiquity and art, you'll love your time spent here. Best of all there's no cost to visit.

Shatin, Chinese University, Hong Kong, Phone: +852-3943-7416.

The Chinese Opera at Ko Shan Theater and New Wing

The Chinese Opera does a fabulous job of evoking the charm and mystery of ancient China. Few other art forms offer so many visual explorations such as distinctive falsetto singing punctuated by gongs, kaleidoscopic, intrinsic costumes, and wonderful symbolism. Enjoy a modern Chinese performance art form, of a traditional performance art. Make sure that the Chinese Opera makes your to do list, because you won't be disappointed.

77 Ko Shan Road, Hung Hom, Kowloon, Hong Kong, Phone: +852-2740-9222.

Feng Shui

Feng shui means wind and water, and it's the ancient Chinese practice of positioning building and objects in harmony with nature to enjoy good fortune. Tons of locals believe that when you have good feng shui you will attract prosperity and keep bad luck at bay. Practitioners are hired when new homes and commercial space is built or bought, which is why you can find the use of feng shui throughout the city. One example can be seen in front of the HSBC Main Building in Central you'll find two famous bronze lions. So while you explore the city watch for the use of Feng Shui. It's everywhere and it's very interesting, No other place in the world is it as obvious.

Observation Wheel

The Hong Kong Observation Wheel offers stunning views of Victoria Harbour from 60-metre high!

33 Man Kwong St, Central

The Hong Kong Observatory Tsim Sha Tsui

On a small hill in Kowloon, you will find the Hong Kong Observatory, which was established way back in 1883. In 1912, it was designated as the Royal Observatory. This two-storey plaster and brick structure has long verandas and arched windows. The operational part of the observatory has been moved to a new location, but the old building still holds the offices for the administration center. It's a great place to visit to learn about the observatory's history. It's very cool seeing just how it got started.

134A Nathan Road, Tsim Sha Tsui, Hong Kong, Phone: +852-2926-8200.

Tung Wah Museum

Originally, the Tung Wah Museum was in the main building of Kwong Wah Hospital, which was the first hospital in Kowloon and the New Territories to provide locals with medical services. The museum combines Chinese architecture and Western architecture and it will tell many stories of interest about the development of this very important local hospital, as well as historical records, publications, and so much more. This is a side of Hong Kong that you aren't going to find from a tourist tour. Lots to learn here!

Kwong Wah Hospital, 25 Waterloo Road, Kowloon, Phone: +852-2770-0867.

Jaa bar *Special mission!*

For over 150 years, Peel Street's steep slope has been challenging unfit tourists and locals. At one time, you would have found colonial quarters but now it's a cultural hotspot. One of the best kept secrets is Jaa bar, an intimate bar, which you will find tucked behind the main street. It's scene from Moulin Rouge, where the drinks are decadent and just a bit daring, and you'll feel at home in no time and maybe even make some friends.

Next to 33 Peel Street (via Gage Street), Central, Hong Kong, Phone: +852-2815 8887.

Mong Kok's Wall of Fame

This MK alleyway has been what has fostered the art scene on the local streets, although it's been illegal for around a decade, although the police tend to ignore it all. The myriad of works springs up over a two block section of wall. One reason it's so popular with the street artists is that coming from Argyle Street you can't even see it. Street artists are some very talented individuals and you won't want to miss seeing this mini gallery of sorts! From one visit to the next new art springs up on top of the old.

Alleyway between Argyle Street and Bute Street, Mong Kok (turn left at 111 Argyle Street).

Hong Kong Museum of History

There's plenty to see here in the full 3 floors of history. In fact, leave yourself a minimum of 4 hours so you can really get connected and get a true understanding of the history and cultural changes that have occurred in Hong Kong. The museum dates back 400 years and moves through the years chronologically. It's easy to navigate and super interesting. It will leave you with a better understanding of the country you are visiting. Admission: HK$10.

100 Chatham Rd S, Tsim Sha Tsui East, Kowloon, Hong Kong, Phone: 852-2724-9042

TO VISIT - What's Happening Festivals Calendar

Cirque de la Symphonie

If you love to watch high wire circus acts you are going to love Cirque de la Symphonie, which is a huge circus complete with a live orchestra. Acrobats, contortionists, and jugglers all perform to a number of tunes. May 11-12 Hong Kong Cultural Center 10 Salisbury Rd, Tsim Sha Tsui Hong Kong. *Tickets range from HK$488 to HK$1888.*

Bruno Mars

If you are a Bruno Mars fan what would be more fun than going all the way to Hong Kong to watch a Bruno mars concert. There's really not much that can be added about Bruno Mars. His concerts never disappoint, and he is one of the most talented performers around. He will be performing at the Cheong Wing Rd, Chek Lap Kok, Lantau Island, Hong Kong, May 12-13, *Tickets range from HK$1200 to HK$1550,*

HK Wall Murals Festival *Special mission!*

HK Walls Murals offer a street art festival. This is the only festival that's dedicated to street art. The festival's hub main area is Tai Ping Shan Street, but you will spot street art on walls throughout the area. Make sure you checkout the alley between Sai Street and Upper Station Street. Make the effort to take this festival in from May on throughout the year.

Chinese Opera Festival

The Chinese Opera Festival is traditional but innovative, presenting performances by the top maestros and virtuosi in the field. This year the program includes Peking, Yue, Kungu, Diaogiang, Puxian, Xiqin, and Pingdiao operas as well as the local Cantonese opera. The Opera House will vary depending on the dates and performance. The festival runs from June 14 to August 12, 2018.

Chinese Opera

Le French May Arts

This is one of the biggest cultural events to take place in Asia offering over 120 programs that are presented over May and June. Le French pays tribute to some of the masters and revisits some of the most iconic pieces. Event Highlights are as follows (But there are many more). Tickets available at URBTIX Phone: +852-3761-6661 and performances run from May 1 to June 30.

«The Painting on the Wall» - The Mystical World of a Chinese Novel by Ballet Preljocaj May 3-4.

«School of Nice» – From Pop Art to Happenings May 3-4.

«School of Nice» – From Pop Art to Happenings May 5-27.

«La Vie en Rose» – June 20.

Great Music 2018

Great Music 2018 features the most well-known artists and art groups performing music from a mix of genres. Performances throughout the year, but here are a few highlights. Tickets available at URBTIX Phone: +852-3761-6661 and you can also find out what's happening where.

Jaap, To The New World

Jaap, Symphony no. 0 from the New World. The esteemed Music Director Jaap van Zweden embarks on his own New York venture, and he's being honored with this American themed program. Runs June 22-23 at the Concert Hall Hong Kong Cultural Center. Tickets available at URBTIX Phone: +852-3761-6661.

Hong Kong Spoken Word Festival

This popular event is where true stories are performed and told in front of a live audience. It celebrates storytelling, poetry, writing, acting, and comedy. It runs over a 2-week period from May 17 to June 2 at various locations.

International Arts Council 2018

This is one of the biggest family arts festivals that Hong Kong has. There's a fantastic array of fun filled arts programs including electroluminescent, ballet, traditional Chinese puppetry, music theater, circus shows, local music performers, and more. Runs from July 6 to August 12 at various venues. Tickets available at URBTIX Phone: +852-3761-6661.

Monkey God Festival

The mischievous Monkey God appeared first in the Ming Dynasty period. In mythology, the Monkey God was born from a mystical stone on the Flowers and Fruit Mountain. Taoist practices provided supernatural powers. The Monkey God Festival is a way to remember the Monkey God and it's an experience you won't soon forget. The date of the festival is September 25, and it will be held at Po Tat Estate, Po Lam Road, Sau Mau Ping, Kowloon.

Monkey King, Monkey Gold Festival, Hong Kong

TO VISIT - Night Clubs & Bars

Visage One

Behind Hollywood Road in the alley you'll find Visage One, an awesome night spot. Benky Chan (owner) combines his love of jazz and haircutting with this mixed venue. During the week hair salon but Saturday nights is jazz night. Best way to find out more is by word of mouth as it's a bit covert.

LG/F, Po Lung Building, behind 93 Hollywood Road (off Shin Hing Street), Central, Phone: 2523-8988.

Lan Kwai Fong (LKF)

Kwai Fong is a great place to party with locals, expats, and tourists alike. This is Hong Kong's most popular night life. Every evening it comes to life.

Central, Hong Kong 00000, China

Lan Kwai Fong, Hong Kong

M Bar *Special mission!*

On Floor 25 of the Mandarin Oriental, you will find the M Bar. Here you'll not only get to see amazing reviews, you can enjoy handcrafted in-house liqueurs and batch spirits.

5 Connaught Rd Central, Hong Kong, Phone: +852-2825-4002

Volar

The legendary Volar is located in the center of Lan Kwai Fong, which is the clubbing street. It has remained on the cutting edge continually reinventing itself over the years with its music and design. Usually they have two rooms on the go so you have music type options. Plus it has a very cool layout and is very futuristic. You won't be disappointed!

44 D'Aguilar St, Central, Hong Kong, Phone: +852-2810-1510.

Ce La Vi

Ce La Vi is one of the top party destinations in Asia, with its sophisticated rooftop vibe, and sleek red interior it's a great place to come dance the night away. Throughout the week, there are different events. Here you can enjoy the sky bar, fine dining restaurant, and pumping club lounge. This is where you come to spend the socialites. You're going to love it!

California Tower, D'Aguilar Street, Central, Hong Kong, Phone: +852-3700-2300

Ce a Vi, D'Aguilar Street, Central, Hong Kong, by Ce la Vi.

Dragon-i

This is where you will find the social elite hanging out – celebrities, CEOs, models, etc. pack the lounge to enjoy a great night. Grab a beer, grab a table, and kick back. The quirky Asian touches include Chinese lanterns. It's dark and chic, with a touch of class! There's a style door policy so don't bother showing up unless you 'dress to impress.'

UG/F, The Centrium, 60 Wyndham St, Hong Kong Tel: +852 3110 1222

Ozone at Ritz Carlton

This is a bit more lounge than club, but there's a live DJ and a minimalist, chill house that's easy to start moving to. The bar is cool with marble with Sci-Fi lighting. It's a cross between a cocktail bar and a pumping night club. If you want prime seating you have to be ready to meet their minimum spend.

Ritz-Carlton Hong Kong, International Commerce Centre, 1 Austin Road, Kowloon, Phone: +852-2263-2263.

TAP The Ale Project

There are plenty of craft breweries and craft beer bars in town, but there aren't many like TAP, where you'll find bottle and draft options continuously rotating with international and local brews. The staff here are passionate about the beer! They've planned their bar bites to match their beer menu. If you love beer, you are going to love it!

G/F 15 Hak Po Street, Mong Kok, Hong Kong, Phone: +852-2468-2010.

Aberdeen Street Social

Whether you've just finished a busy day of shopping or are just looking for a weekend out, the Aberdeen Street Social is perfect for a bite to eat and a drink, whether it's lunch or dinner. Enjoy their garden or balcony seating and take in the colorful building.

G/F, JPC, PMQ, 35 Aberdeen St, Central, Hong Kong, Phone: +852-2866-0300

Drunkerland

Drunkerland offers more than 100 brews from across the UK, US, Japan, and Belgium, as well as their very own Hong Kong brew. Come enjoy a relaxed atmosphere and kick back.

27 Ngan Mok St, Tin Hau, Hong Kong, Phone: +852=3702-1841

Drunkerland, Hong Kong

TO VISIT - NOT Tourist Places (the Advice of Locals)

Jade Market & Jade Street

In the Chinese culture jade has long been associated with longevity and health, and the Jade Market has all kinds of jade goods, jade jewelry, jade accessories, well pretty much anything jade that local vendors are selling. You never know what unusual find you'll discover and you'll definitely have fun strolling through the market.

Junction of Kansu Street and Battery Street, Yau Ma Tei, Kowloon

The Jade Market

Saddle Up for Horse Racing at Happy Valley Racecourse *Special mission!*

Whether you love the game, love to socialize, or love the beer, there is no question that the locals love their race track and so will you. There are tons of opportunities here to bet on the races, but Wednesday nights are considered the hottest ticket! Make it part of your Hong Kong vacation and go home with a new love for horse racing in Hong Kong.

Take a Ride on the Ding-Ding

Hong Kong's tram is affectionately called the Ding-Ding, because of their bells, and they are a city icon, and a main method of public transportation. You'll get on the back and then exit by the front and pay the driver then. Adult HK$2.30, Child K$1.20, Senior K$1.10, 4 day pass K$34.00

The House of Siren

This is a gem in more than one way. Yes, it's a hidden gem, but it's also, where you will find gems sewn into the 300 costumes that are for rent. It's been open since 1996 and the locals love to rent their costumes here. The kinds of costumes you get to see plus the dramatically decorated store are worth the visit even when you aren't in the market to rent a costume, be sure to check it out, you may never see anything like it again.

AC *LG/F, Carlos Court, 64 Robinson Road (entrance behind building), Central, Phone: 2530-2371.*

Yuen Po Street Bird Garden

Songbird supporters love to hang out at the Yuen Po Street Bird Garden has been designed as a traditional Chinese garden. There are all kinds of stalls each selling their own unique bird related items, whether it's beautiful bamboo cages, exotic birds, or bird care items. Sure as a tourist, you won't likely be taking home any exotic birds, but you are going to love the experience.

Yuen Po Street, Prince Edward, Kowloon, Phone: +852-2302-1762.

Old School Barber Shop *Special mission!*

This vintage barber has been serving locals for 50 years in a tiny alley between Shing Wong Street and Hollywood Road, right beside a loo. Even with the construction boom around it, this shop has remained unchanged. It still has old fashioned barber chairs, with great prices. Check it out and get your very own Old School cut.

Corner of Hollywood Road and Shing Wong Street, Central.

Beatniks

If you peer down the dimly lit alley on the Graham Street side, you'll notice the Beatniks store, with all its vintage collectibles, clothes, and accessories. The store is like a time capsule with things like a woven tapestry of Elvis on the wall, or The Beatles memorabilia. Take a walk back in time and who knows what treasure you'll find to take home with you. The locals love this little gem and they try to keep it their own secret.

Behind 31 Staunton Street, Central, Phone: 2881-7153.

Yick Fat Building

Just off King's Road you'll find the Yick Fat building, which is a large residential complex where you'll find apartments atop massage parlors, independent launderettes, and more. When you wonder down the alley where it connects to Quarry Bay Street you'll discover the courtyard of the complex, and some of the most amazing architecture. The paints peeling off the walls, and the canopies are tired, a stark contrast to the clean, glossy towers only a block away. Check it out! The locals love the little shops and courtyard, which made notoriety with the Transformer movie.

Yick Fat Building Courtyard, between Yau Man Street and Quarry Bay Street, Quarry Bay.

Play Club

This nightclub is very popular with the locals and the expats elitists. It's over 6000 square feet, and the interior is very chic. It's divided into sections designed so that guests can decide what their experience will be. It could be the dance floor, or maybe you need some pampering in the Dom Perignon Champagne Lounge where you'll be treated like a VIP. You never know whom you might run into. Find out for yourself why the locals love it!

On Hing Building, 1 On Hing Terrace, Central, Phone: +852-2525-1318.

Temple Street Night Market *Special mission!*

This is another place you must visit. It's the only night market left in Hong Kong and the locals love it. Here you can find goods, electronics, eclectic foods, clothing, jade, and more. There's even a fortune teller when you need a break from your shopping, or listen to the music.

Temple St, Yau Ma Tei, Hong Kong.

Kitchenware Galore

Locals love these shops because you can find anything you need for in the kitchen for great prices and what's even more entertaining is the size ranges some of this stuff is available in. Think about a cutting board that is 100 times the size of the one you have. Yes from mini to giant, you'll see kitchenware like never before.

Shanghai Street, Hong Kong

Sham Shui Po

This is cheapest market in Hong Kong, which is why you'll find so many locals hanging out here. Whether you need an LED lamp, some new electronics, or toys for the kids, you can find it all here. There are tons of vendors to choose from selling everything imaginable.

Located in north-west Kowloon Peninsula, east of Cheung Sha Wan, south of Shek Kip Mei, and north of Tai Kok Tsui.

TO DO - Outdoor Adventures and Nature

Ride a Glass Bottom Gondola

Enjoy the stunning views and sheer beauty on the Ngong Ping 360 Skyrail cable car that will take you all the way to the giant Tian Tan Buddha. The glass bottom gondola will cost you a little more but it's worth it for visitors who will get a unique view of Lantau Island, unless you have a fear of heights.

Lantau Island, Hong Kong, Phone: +852-3666-0606

Hike to The Peak *Special mission!*

There are tons of hiking trails in Honk Kong and you should take the time to explore some of them. One of the best panoramas can be seen hiking The Peak. There are options like The Peak Circle Walk, which is more leisure, or you can go for the more challenging hike up The Peak. What a rush!

View of Victoria Harbor from the Peak

Repulse Bay

Repulse Bay beach is one of the most popular Hong Kong beaches. You will also get to enjoy some traditional Chinese architecture with its colonial influence at the Hong Kong Life Saving Society Clubhouse. It's a win-win, fabulous time on the beach and fabulous dining after.

South of Taiping Mountain, South District, Hong Kong, China

Dragon Back Hike *Special mission!*

If you are ready for an escape from the busy city and some exercise, this popular trail will do both while providing you with great views of Mount Collinson, Big Wave Bay, and more. It's a fairly easy hike so no need to be in top notch shape.

Hong Kong, Shek O, Dragon's Back

Dolphin Watching Tour

What if you could see pink dolphins in their natural habitat? Well you can! The Lung Kwu Chau Marine Park and Sha Chau offer pink dolphin watching and you'll enjoy some great scenery too. What a great memory to take home with you!

1528A, Star House, Tsim Sha Tsui, Kowloon, Phone: +852-2984-1414.

Big Wave Beach *Special mission!*

You might be surprised to discover how many great beaches Hong Kong has, where you can bask in the sun, swim, and relax. The waves gently roll in to a cover that's u shaped. Big Wave Beach is a great beach to combine the city and beach. You're going to love it!

Big Wave Bay Road, Shek O, Hong Kong Island, Phone: +852-2809-4558

Sai Kung West Country Park

Sai Kung West Country Park is a great place to enjoy nature with its dense exotic vegetation, lovely wild azaleas, rhododendrons, and other flowers. There is also the Ma On Shan hike where you'll enjoy some superb views. Make sure that you visit the Tin Hau Temple.

1 Sai Kung Hoi Pong St, Hong Kong, Phone: +852-9187-8641.

Heli services Tours

Heli services offers four main tours and they are the only flight seeing service in Hong Kong. Usually the MD902 Explorer is used for the tours, which seats seven. There's the Geopark Experience, Kowloon Experience, Hong Kong Island Experience, and a 15 minute short flight around Hong Kong. What a great way to see Hong Kong and area from a bird's eye view.

Booking enquiry: +852-2802-0200 or chp@heliservices.com.hk

Tram up to The Peak

Make sure that you take a ride on the historic Peak Tram, which runs continuously from the early hours to midnight. You have lots of time to check out the views as you climb to the top of the famous mountain.

Central, Hong Kong, Phone: +852-2522-0922

Tram heading up to The Peak, Hong Kong

Old Town Central

Under the stunning Central skyline, you can enjoy art, food, history, and culture that flourish in the oldest neighborhood. Here is where the present meets the past, innovation meets tradition, and tranquility meets excitement. There are five different routes you can take to discover Hong Kong's colorful history, or you can wander around yourself. Be sure to explore the many shops in Old Town.

TO TASTE - Local Food &Cuisine

Qinghai Tibetan Noodles *Special mission!*

Qinghai is one stop you won't want to miss out on. Their Tibetan noodles are so delicious, but they also offer tons of other great dishes – it's like having a full range of the best restaurants under one room including the likes of a French Bistro, a Malaysian restaurant, and a funky Singapore diner, and more, which is why you'll find the locals hanging out here.

27 Kam Ping St, North Point, Hong Kong, Phone: +852-215-0506.

Hung Fook Seafood Hot Pot

If you are looking for down to earth local cuisine, you'll want to check out this restaurant. It's tucked down a long alleyway that looks a bit shady, but don't let that scare you off! As you get near you'll get the delicious smells from the various dishes wafting your way, drawing you in. Trust me, you won't be able to resist. You'll be talking about Hung Fook for months to come.

86 Lok Shan Road, To Kwa Wan, Hong Kong

Tim Ho Wan

When in Hong Kong, eat with the locals and enjoy the dim sum at Tim Ho Wan, which is not going to disappoint you. Their most famous dish is their mouthwatering barbecue pork baked bun, which the locals call char siu bao, and don't be surprised when you find yourself addicted to this great dish. Be sure to check out the rest of the menu too!

Olympia City 2, 18 Hoi Ting Rd, West Kowloon, Hong Kong, Phone: +852-2332-2896.

Hoover Cake Shop

The locals love the egg tarts that Hoover Cake shop offers! These little tarts with their flaky pie crust and delicious egg custard are a staple in Hong Kong, and Hoover makes some of the best! Don't let the run-down neighborhood keep you away. It certainly doesn't keep the wealthy away that stop by regularly to pick up boxes of egg tarts.

136 Nga Tsin Wai Rd Kowloon City, Hong Kong, Phone: +852-2382-0383.

Haiphong Road Temporary Market Noodle Stall

A visit to Hong Kong wouldn't be complete without a visit to the noodle stall tucked away in the Haiphong Road Temporary Market, which actually has been around for over 30 years. Take as stroll through the market past the many vendors until you come across customers that are sitting eating delicious beef balls and noodles in bright orange bowls using yellow spoons – you can't miss it! They are perfect and it's what keeps the locals coming back for more!

Haiphong Road Temporary Market, 390 Haiphong Road, Tsim Sha Tsui, Phone: +852-2376-1179.

Cha Chaan Teng (Tea Café)

Since 1967, Cha Chaan Teng has been serving locals and now they have dozens of café's throughout Hong Kong. If you want the comfort foods locals love, you'll want to stop by and enjoy the Tsui Wah or one of the other delicious dishes. Make sure you enjoy a cup of sweetened milk tea (hot or cold) while you're there!

Branches include GF-2F, 15-19 Wellington Street, Central, Phone: +852-2525-6338.

Under Bridge Spicy Crab Restaurant

Typhoon shelter crab dish is a Hong Kong original, named after the coves where fishermen took shelter if they were caught in stormy weather. Since the boat facilities were limited, the fishermen would cook the fresh crab they caught in black beans, spring onions, chili peppers, and tons of garlic, then serve with either rice or congee, and a beer. The original Under Bridge Spicy Crab is the most basic of their restaurants providing a unique dining experience. Plastic sheets are draped over the tables and when you are done the grab shells and the plastic are gathered and tossed.

The original branch is at 429 Lockhart Road, Causeway Bay, Phone: +852-2573-7698. Many other branches.

ABC Kitchen

Hong Kong food markets are lined with stall where you eat sitting on stools at folding tables, but the ABC Kitchen is different. It's turned up the class a little, with red and white check tablecloths, and a bottle of wine on the table. Enjoy one of the many traditional Chinese meals, including their famous roast suckling pig, braised lamb shank, beef Wellington, and dessert soufflés. They also offer a few non-Chinese meals. This restaurant has some of the best food around. Make sure to put it on your list!

1F Queen Street Cooked Food Market, 38 Des Voeux Road West, Sheung Wan, Phone: +852-9278-8227.

Lin Heung Tea House

The Lin Heung Tea House has been around since 1920 and some of the customers and servers look like they may have been there from the beginning. This is one of the few restaurants left where the dim sum is served on a trolley cart. Dinner is the best! They serve some great old fashion dishes like pan fried minced pork patties. Come enjoy!

160-164 Wellington Street, Central, Hong Kong, Phone: +852-2544-4556.

Ma Sa Restaurant

When in Hong Kong you simply must have at least one meal of spam and egg rice, an authentic cha chaan teng dish, and now you get this simple dish at its best served to perfection. Cheap and so delicious!

G/F, 23 Hillier St, Sheung Wan, Hong Kong, Phone: +852-2545-9026.

Ham & Sherry

No, that's not the name of a drink, it's the name of a tapas bar – yes, locals sometimes like something different from Cantonese food or dim sum, and that's what makes this a hot spot. Try the Iberico ham – you'll love it!

1-7 Ship St, Wan Chai, Hong Kong, Phone: +852-2555-0628.

Tsui Wah Restaurant

Locals have either been to or heard of Tsui Wah Restaurant. Not only does it offer good food, it is open 24-hours, and it's conveniently located near some of the more popular nightlife spots.

Tsui Wah Restaurant, 15 Wellington Street, Central, Hong Kong, Phone: +852-2542-2288.

Tasty Congee & Noodle Wantun Shop

This busy little shop is popular with the locals, serving top quality Chinese cuisine, with congee and wanton noodles being their specialty items. Their location is also one of the reasons it's so popular. It's come a long way from its first shop in the 1940s, which was a street food stall.

Tasty Congee and Noodle Wantun Shop, IFC, Central, Hong Kong, Phone: +852-2295-0505.

Tai Ping Koon Restaurant

Back in 1860 in China (yes you read that right), the first Tai Ping Koon Restaurant opened. Tai Ping Koon is unique in that it offers Chinese style Western food, which includes foods like Portuguese baked chicken, and French soufflé Hong Kong style for the most discerning palates.

Tai Ping Koon, 6 Pak Sha Road, Causeway Bay, Hong Kong, Phone: +852-2576-9196, or 60 Stanley Street, Central, Hong Kong, Phone: +852-2899-2780.

Hunan Garden Restaurant

This popular restaurant specializes in cuisine from the Chinese province of Hunan, you can enjoy something for every taste bud, from non-spicy to mildly spicy to super-hot for those that love the heat, all clearly marked on the restaurant. Come check out this local hangout and make reservations so you are not disappointed.

Hunan Garden, 14 Tai Koo Wan Road, Hong Kong, Phone: +852-3691-9928.

Affordable Cool Cafes and Restaurants

Open-door Café and Courtyard

The character and individuality of the Open-door Café and Courtyard are adored. Behind the frosted glass doors, a nice quiet space is available, it hosts independent events and artworks, and of course, there's the serene terrace to enjoy. So come take a breather and enjoy a cup of honey processed coffee and a gluten free treat.

120 Connaught Rd W, Sai Ying Pun, Hong Kong, Phone: +852-3460-3880.

Café Corridor

Initially this was the place 'to be' to enjoy a delicious sweet treat and great cup of coffee, but today, punters love this café because of the secret terrace found out back. Just past the innocent metal door, you'll find a few small tables, which is a great place to relax and get away from the overstimulation around Time Square.

26A Russell St, Causeway Bay, Hong Kong, Phone: +852-2892-2927.

Sun Thai Restaurant

Here you'll get to enjoy some delicious authentic Thai food at an affordable price, in a swanky setting. Whether you are by yourself, part of a large group, with or without kids, they have you covered. Great food that includes the red and green curries to local seafood with a Thai twist. Recommendations suggested on weekends.

2F, W Square, 318 Hennessey Road, Wan Chai, Hong Kong, Phone: +852-2827-8877.

Yao Lei

About one block from Tiffany & Co's Causeway Bay branch, you will find the pop up breakfast café Yao Lei, which is very special. You'll find it down the tiny alley that cuts through from Tang Lung Street to Russell Street, and it's a popular stop with the locals. It opens at 6 AM and closes around 2 PM. When closed, you'll never know it was there. A warning there's not English menu, only Chinese.

Between Tang Lung Street and Russell Street, Causeway Bay, Hong Kong.

Jumbo Kingdom *Special mission!*

At the famous Aberdeen pier on Hong Kong Island, you'll find this huge floating restaurant called the Jumbo Kingdom. Open since 1976, this entertainment floating empire draws 30+ million visitors a year, including movie stars and royalty.

Shum Wan Pier Drive, Wong Chuk Hang, Aberdeen, Hong Kong Tel: Phone: +852-2553-9111.

Arcane

In Central in the dense urban landscape, you'll find Arcane wedged between two buildings. Shane Osborn, an award winning chef, offers a garden sanctuary that is European inspired. Eat and drink in this lush green space in this very private space.

3/F, 18 On Lan St, Central, Phone: 852-2728-0178.

Tung Po

On the second floor of the Java Road wet market you'll find the Tung Po, a seafood restaurant ran by owner Robby Cheung, who has made his restaurant famous with his white rubber wellies and wacky hairstyles. As night arrives, the music gets louder and customers sing along. Enjoy a very tasty meal, whether that's the razor clams in black bean sauce, deep fried pig's trotters, squid ink pasta with cuttlefish balls, or something else. Enjoy the friendly atmosphere and a beer in a bowl.

2F Java Road Municipal Services Building, 99 Java Road, North Point, Phone: +852-288-5224.

Piggy Grill

At the Piggy Grill, you'll enjoy piglets roasted over an open flame, and perfectly cooked. If suckling pig isn't your idea of a good meal, don't worry because they offer many other great dishes, including roast duck and seafood. Beer is served in a bowl and the décor is basic, but the food is 'to die for!'

Shop 1, 17 Shun Ning Road, Sham Shui Po, Phone: +852-2194-8188.

Kau Kee

Half of the charm here is the grumpy staff. There menu is small, but their food is delicious. Beef brisket, beef tendon, and various noodles are offered. Don't expect any ambience. You'll sit on unpadded stools around a glass covered table. The staff is abrupt and rude to everyone so don't take it personally.

21 Gough Street, Central, Hong Kong, +852-2850-5967.

Kau Kee Restaurant Central Hong Kong

9 ¾ Cafe

Yes 9 ¾ Café is an odd name, but this is a themed café around Harry Potter, so if you are a Potter fan, you'll understand. Potterheads have serious magical potions all paying respect to J.K. Rowling. As a Harry Potter fan, this café is everything you could want and dream of with genuine Harry Potter merchandise. 9 ¾ Café's Western dishes are named after characters and mythical themes, like the Polyjuice Potion or the Order of the Phoenix. Call ahead to book your spot.

4/F, Prosper Commercial Building, 9 Yin Chong Street, Mong Kok, Phone: +852- 9432-6555.

The Cat Store

In a mixed residential commercial building in Causeway Bay tucked deep inside the 3rd floor you'll discover this quirky store and café where 11 resident cats live that love to be loved. To go with the live cats, there are tons of decorations, photos, murals, lighting, and just about anything you can think of that can be cat fun. The prices are reasonable, the food is good, the cats are fun, and you can even take a cat trinket home with you from the store.

3D Po Ming Building, Foo Ming Street, Causeway Bay, Hong Kong, Phone: +852-2710-9953

Enjoying a meal at the Cat Store with cat posing for picture

TO BUY - Local and Authentic Souvenirs

Traditional Chinese Clothing

Chinese traditional dress is called Cheongsam, and it emerged in the 1920s. It is a great souvenir for women. For the men the changshan or mao suit is perfect. It's stylish and elegant and you can wear it when you return home, all the while bringing something memorable home.

Chinese Art

What could be better than taking home an aesthetic higher value piece of Chinese art, which will stand out in your home décor and always remind you of your holiday to Hong Kong. It could be porcelain, pottery, sculpture, or a painting, so keep your eyes open. Stanley Market, Hollywood Road and Temple Street Night Market are great places to buy Chinese Art.

Chinese Art, Hong Kong

Chinese Antiques

China has a long history and there are plenty of oriental antiques that you might find that are small enough to take home, and what a great way to remember your trip. Every time you look at it, you'll be reminded of your Hong Kong vacation. Upper Lascar Row and Stanley market are good places to discover these antiques.

Goods of Desire

This might not be a term you are familiar with, but Goods of Desire have become very sought after by travelers because of their humor. When you enter Goods of Desire, you'll discover all kinds of cool kitsch that you can take home with you - everything from bags to stationary, to silk items. 35 Aberdeen Street and 48 Hollywood Road are where you can begin your search for Goods of Desire.

Hong Kong Snacks

Snacks might not be a souvenir you were thinking of bringing home with you but it's practical and who doesn't enjoy snacks, so there definitely won't be any waste. Your snack choices are many whether its egg rolls or Pretz shark fin. Make sure you can take your choices back into your country.

Chinese Tea

The Chinese love their teas and what a perfect souvenir to bring home with you. It's healthy, tasty, and memorable. You can choose from many flavors, green teas, oolong teas, black teas, and white teas.

Chinese Tea and other foods, Hong Kong

Porcelain Products

When it comes to porcelain, blue and white wares are very popular in Hong Kong and they make a great souvenir to bring home with you too. Choose an antique dating back to the 9th century or something more modern. You can find porcelain at Temple Street, Stanley Market, and King Tak Hong Porcelain Company.

Jade

Jade is a big part of Chinese culture and it makes a wonderful souvenir. Honk Kong has their own jade industry. Choose from figurines, jewelry, ornaments, furniture, etc. You can buy both real and synthetic jade depending on your budget.

Dried Seafood *Special mission!*

Dried seafood is an age-old tradition and there is a wide assortment of choices in Hong Kong. Sea cucumber, scallop, abalone, etc. are excellent choices for soup and stir fries. There's nothing like eating your souvenir.

Dried Seafood Hong Kong

Custom Name Seals

Name seals are a big part of Chinese history and now you can have your very own custom name seal, where your name is translated to Chinese. What a fantastic souvenir that never gets old. They are made from jade, soapstone, ivory, or some other cool material and have cultural significance. You can get these at Man Wa Lane Chop Alley or on the Antique Street.

TO STAY - the Best Unusual Hotels and Hostels

Conrad Hong Kong

Located in the heart of Hong Kong Island, you will find the Conrad on top of the luxurious Pacific Place shopping mall with designer boutiques and great restaurant options. It's a great place to be inspired with all the hi tech amenities. Top notch yet a little different.

88 Queensway, Admiralty, Hong Kong, Phone: +852-2521-3838.

Sheer luxury second to none at this five star hotel with an incredible spa over two floors, great dining options, hi tech meeting areas, and artistic rooms. An experience like no other. Both rooms and suites are available.

5 Connaught Road Central, Phone: +852-2522-0111.

Hong Kong Disneyland Hotel *Special mission!*

This 4 star hotel is close to Hong Kong Disneyland and offers air conditioned guest rooms, with many amenities. There are Disney characters around the hotel adding an unusual but fun twist to the stay. Kids love it!

Magic Rd, Lantau Island, Hong Kong, Phone: +852-3510-6000.

Island Shangri-La Hotel

At the heart of the city, soaring way above, you'll feel like you are in heaven in this impressive 56 story hotel with 565 guest rooms all exquisitely designed. It's unusual to get this high above but it provides for spectacular views of both the harbor and the Peak. This urban sanctuary is like no other!

Pacific Place, Supreme Ct Rd, Central, Hong Kong, Phone: +852-2877-3838.

Island Shangri La, Hong Kong

Kowloon Shangri-La

This is the perfect place to unwind and enjoy some mouth-watering cuisine. It's unusual for a hotel to be so close to a market but Temple Street Market is right there and you can enjoy some excellent shopping that can offer quality with bargain basement prices.

64 Mody Rd, Tsim Sha Tsui East, Hong Kong, Phone: +852-2721-2111.

Dragon Hostel

Located close to metro and near the center of the shopping street you can shop until midnight no matter what night you feel the urge. Food is just a few minutes away. This hostel is perfect when you just need a place to sleep. It's affordable and clean.

Room 707 /F Hong Kong, Argyle St, Mong Kok, Hong Kong, Phone: +852-2395-0577

Urban Pack

Urban Pack is in a great location next to an MRT stop and with an amazing view of Kowloon Park. It's a small room, but it's clean and you have everything you need. The hosts are always busy setting up fun things to do for their guests, and making recommendations. Best of all it's affordable!

1410, 14/F, Hai Phong Mansion, 53 Hai Phong Road, Tsim Sha Tsui, Tsim Sha Tsui, Hong Kong. Phone: +852-2732-2271

Grand Hyatt

The Grand Hyatt is adjacent to the Convention & Exhibition Center and offers stunning views of the famous Harbor. With 545 rooms, there's something right for you, and these days it's unusual to have your own personal butler. On the 11th floor is a heated pool and fitness studio, and something you don't see very often, a 400 meter jogging path inside.

1 Harbour Rd, Wan Chai, Hong Kong, Phone: +852-2588-1234.

The Langham

The timeless European elegance offers you personalized services, world class cuisine, and a complimentary third night. Crystal glassware, Wedgwood chinaware, British mini bars, Nespresso machines, and so much more. It's unlike any other hotel with its Chuan Body + Soul 604 square meter wellness sanctuary that's based on the five elements – wood, earth, water, metal, and fire.

8 Peking Rd, Tsim Sha Tsui, Hong Kong, Phone: +852-2375-1133.

Intercontinental Hotel

This is considered one of the most prestigious hotels for gala balls, high end business meetings, glamorous weddings, and more. It offers 500 opulent rooms and a 7000 square foot presidential suite, which is very unusual. It has everything you could possibly want, but be prepared to bring your credit card, as it doesn't come cheap!

18 Salisbury Rd, Tsim Sha Tsui, Hong Kong, Phone: +852-2721-1211.

The intercontinental Hong Kong Hotel

Printed in Great Britain
by Amazon